A HIGHER CALLING

Moving Forward in Your Walk with God

ELDER SHANNON
FITZGERALD THOMAS

A HIGHER CALLING: MOVING FORWARD IN YOUR WALK WITH GOD

Copyright © 2021 Elder Shannon Fitzgerald Thomas

Library of Congress Control Number: 2019054242

TABLE OF CONTENTS

FOREWORD v

ACKNOWLEDGMENTS vii

INTRODUCTION ix

CHAPTER 1: From Darkness to Light 1

CHAPTER 2: Receiving the Spirit 5

CHAPTER 3: Hearing His Voice 13

CHAPTER 4: A Call to Obedience 19

CHAPTER 5: Cleaning out the Closet 25

CHAPTER 6: A Call to Service 31

CHAPTER 7: Personal Instructions 37

CHAPTER 8: A Call to Service 41

CONCLUSION: A Higher Calling 53

FOREWORD

As we walk this Christian life following the Savior and His teaching, we sometimes tend to come into a strange area when we think that we have reached as far as we can on this side of salvation. But I have come to the understanding that there is a higher calling.

> *"I press toward the mark for the prize of the high calling of God in Christ Jesus."* (PHILIPPIANS 3:14)

There is a place in Christ Jesus that only one who presses can enter into. New Testament Christians are not mediocre Christians—they are a humble powerhouse; not in word only, but in a living way.

> *"Blessed are they that hunger and thirst for righteousness for they shall be filled!"* (MATTHEW 5:6)

ACKNOWLEDGMENTS

I would like to thank my parents for the example of life and love they set for me.

I would like to thank my beloved wife for praying with me and supporting me.

I would also like to thank my children—Dave, Ginelle, Carlos, and John—for being so loving and understanding.

And I especially thank the Lord Jesus for giving His life and redeeming my soul.

INTRODUCTION

I am Shannon Thomas. I was born in Tuscaloosa, Alabama. I joined the Army after high school. I am a Desert Storm veteran.

In July 1992, the Lord Jesus Christ put a vision into my heart to spread His Gospel all over the world. I began to seek God in a fierce way. I completed research on different denominations of Christianity and different religions entirely. I visited a variety of churches on my quest.

That November, I had a dream that I was battling the devil, and he was winning. He was taking over houses, people, and churches. Suddenly, a voice told me to say, "In the Name of Jesus," so I did. Coincidentally, the devil stopped his attacks. The voice spoke to me again. He said He was going to do a new thing in me, and that I was to move to Birmingham, Alabama. Immediately, I moved to Birmingham. I began to attend The Lord Jesus Christ Church in Ensley. The pastor was Apostle Eric Smith. He preached about the power of God and how to live a holy life. The presence of God manifested there constantly through miracles and signs of the Holy Ghost.

At the time, the Holy Ghost spoke to me about bringing the churches together in Jesus' Name. He told me to do a series of revivals around the city, state, and country, and to call them "Breaking Down the Barrier Crusades." These revivals would call every Christian to be aware of the coming of Jesus and to notice the signs.

This is the first of many books the Holy Ghost has birthed into my spirit to help the body of Christ refocus their vision.

CHAPTER 1

From Darkness to Light

As a young child I was brought up in the church. My mother would send all of us to church every Sunday. I always enjoyed going to church. I went for three reasons: food, music, and money. The food was always delicious and the music made me happy. And before we left for church, Moms would give us money to give to the church and to also go to the Pink Store on the way home. So really, I was not seeking Jesus or the church for Jesus but for the benefits. Me and my four brothers and three sisters sang in a kind of community choir. We sang in churches and at the YMCA, and the people would say how good we were dressed and how nice we looked.

We always knew our Bible verses and all the key words for the day. For example:

> *"Whatsoever you ask in the Name of Jesus you could get."* (JOHN 14:13)

I remember one day my sister Sheila and I were going to school and we had to cross a ditch to get there. It had a very narrow bridge and Sheila was afraid to cross and I remembered that scripture and I said, "Sheila whatever you ask in Jesus Name you can do." So I said, "In the Name of Jesus, let us cross this bridge," and we did it. We still smile about that now.

I got baptized the first time when I was 8 years old because I thought it was the right thing to do. So, after I heard the altar call, I went up to be baptized and "accept Christ," not really understanding what I was doing. Back then they would have you repeat the Sinner's Prayer and say that you accept Jesus as your Lord and you got baptized the same day.

As I grew older, I went to church but did not really learn anything. I was just going through the motions. That is when I used church as a way to be self-justified by saying, "At least I go to church." I also heard you can do anything as long as you ask the Lord's forgiveness before or after you do it. Imagine—I could have my cake and eat it too.

When I graduated from high school, I joined the Army and drifted further from the church, but still asked the Lord to forgive me every night.

I remember one summer my Aunt Dolly came to visit from Gary, Indiana. She called all the relatives over and we had prayer and service. I was about 10 years old, and she said to me that the Lord wanted me to say the first prayer. I was very surprised that the Lord would even speak to me personally or that He even knew me. My mother told me to say the Lord's Prayer, so I did.

The Lord not only knew us, but wanted to build a relationship with us. The Word of God says in John, the 15th chapter:

> *"You are no longer servants, but His friends."*
> (JOHN 15:15)

Abraham was even called a friend of God in Genesis 18:1-8.

Some Christians believe that there is no way for you to ever do what the Bible says, so we will just have to do the best we can until the Lord comes back, and then we will be able to do it. But the Word of God says that

> *"Whosoever has this hope in Him should purify even as He is."* (1 JOHN 3:3)

I remember going to a house service, and a prophetess was there with her husband. She looked at me and told me the Lord wanted me to preach the Gospel.

I said within myself, *Lord if that's your will, let her tell me again.*

Immediately, she turned around and told me again. She told me the same thing on four separate occasions.

One night after drinking as much as I could, I had a headache. But for some reason, I remembered those key scriptures:

"If you ask anything in the name of Jesus you can get it." (JOHN 14:14)

So, I said sarcastically, "In the Name of Jesus, make this headache stop." And to my surprise it stopped! I began to feel so dirty and unworthy to have asked for the Lord to heal me. So, in the Name of Jesus I asked that He would forgive my sins, and I felt relieved. Then I even went a step further. After drinking beer, liquor, and wine, and smoking cigarettes, I asked the Lord to take the taste of alcohol and nicotine out of my mouth. As soon as I finished praying the prayer, the physical tastes left my mouth!

It was amazing!—so amazing that I went back to where I used to hang out with my friends and told them about what the Lord had done for me. One of my friends told me that I had lost my mind; that broke my heart. After being delivered, the Lord began to reveal Himself to me. The church songs that we used to sing began to have meaning to me. When I read the Bible, I began to feel lonely. The only comfort I got was from reading the Word, but that was only temporary.

I began to go to every church that I knew was open. I prayed, "Lord, I wish I could have church every day." I knew that I was saved, but I also knew that there was something missing—it was something or some place in God that I had not yet reached. So, I began to search the scriptures. I had a hunger for the Word of God; I could not get enough. Being around church folks seemed to fill some of my missing void, but it did not completely fill it. Something was still missing.

CHAPTER 2

Receiving the Spirit

"Blessed are they that hunger and thirst for righteousness and ye shall be filled." (MATTHEW 5:6)

After accepting Christ as Lord of your life, there is another step in Christ—to receive His Spirit. There are many Christians who start off right but never get their hunger sated or their void filled, so they substitute it with just raw religion, tradition, or the Word. The letter killeth, but the spirit brings it to life.

Jesus declared that the time was coming, and now is that time. The true worshiper will worship in spirit and in truth (John 4:23). He also said that, except if you be born again, you can't enter the kingdom of God—you need the birth of the water and the spirit (John 3:1-7).

Confessing Jesus as Lord but not accepting His Spirit is like accepting a new car without the engine. The Spirit of God gives you the power to do the Will of God. It gives you the personal information about the Word of God that only He can reveal. It keeps you in tune to the voice of God and gives you the understanding of exactly what God means in His Word.

Some people believe that only certain Christians receive the Spirit of God while some do not. But the Spirit of God is for every born-again believer. Some Christians believe that only special Christians—pastors, evangelists, prophets, or teachers—*need* to receive the Spirit of God. But there is potential for any Christian to hold any of these offices. In order to understand the Word of God, you need the Spirit of God. It is not only available to every Christian—it is a necessary force walk this Christian life. It is very hard to live an effective, victorious Christian life without the Spirit of God. The Spirit of God will teach you the Word of God from every angle and lead you into all truths (John 16:13).

Jesus said,

> *"My Word is Spirit and life."* (JOHN 6:63)

So, in order to read the Spirit in life or the Word of God, you need to have the Spirit and life. The Word of God says in 1 John 5:7,

> *"For there are three that bear record in heaven—the Father, the Word, and the Holy Ghost—and these three are one."*

After receiving the Spirit of God, the Word of God comes alive, your understanding grows, and the presence of God is manifest to you like you can't imagine. Jesus said,

"I am the way the truth and the life." (JOHN 14:6)

There is a definition of truth as being the highest form of reality. The reality of God is in His Spirit. The thing that identifies you, your thoughts, ideals, likes, and character is your spirit. So, in order to understand God's character, you need to have His Spirit. In order to know the depth of His love for us, you must have His Spirit. That is why Jesus told Nicodemus that except if ye be born again, you can't see the Kingdom of God. (John 3:3)

If you cannot identify with someone or understand the type of person they are, you may misunderstand what they are saying or the intent of their words. For example, if I were to say, "That shirt you have on is bad," you might misinterpret what I said unless you knew my intent. This is especially true today, when "bad" can mean "good" in some conversations. We need the Spirit of God. God's character is in His Word.

Some people think when you have the Spirit of God or the Holy Ghost, you speak in tongues. Although that is one piece of evidence of having received the Holy Ghost, it is not the only one. Jesus said,

"You shall know them by their fruit" (MATTHEW 7:16)

And the fruit of the Spirit is love, joy, peace, goodness, meekness, temperance, longsuffering, faith, and gentleness (Galatians 5:22, 23). When you see true Christians, they should have these fruit manifesting in their lives. But, not stopping there, Jesus said,

> *"And these signs shall follow them—that believe. In my name, they shall cast out devils, they shall speak with new tongues, if they drink anything deadly, it will not hurt them. They shall lay hands on the sick, and they shall recover."* (MARK 16:11)

Every Christian is called to have these fruit and the power to put the enemy on the run. The more you yield yourself to the Spirit of God, the more you will receive.

The Spirit of God is important in this Christian walk, but God will not force Himself upon you; the Spirit of God has to be received. When it comes to receiving the Spirit of God, there are people who don't understand how or why He is needed in their life. They let fear of the unknown take over and block them from receiving. The way you receive the Holy Ghost or the Spirit of God is by faith. Believe and receive, and ye shall have; ask it shall be given; seek ye shall find; knock, and the door shall be open. (Matthew 7:7) *For everyone who asks receives!*

Jesus said in John 16:24,

> *"Hitherto have ye asked nothing in my name: ask, and ye shall receive, that your joy may be full."*

The Word of God says in Romans 8:9-10,

> *"Now, if any man have not the Spirit of Christ, he is none of His. And if Christ be in you the body is dead because of sin, but the Spirit is life because of righteousness."*

In Romans 8:14 and 16, we learn:

> *"For as many that are led by the Spirit if God, they are the Sons of God... The Spirit itself bears witness that we are the Children of God."*

How can you be led by the Spirit of God if you have not received Him? If you are not sure if you have received Him, you have not. Take a moment and ask the Lord to baptize you with His Spirit.

Have you ever gone on your knees to pray and not known exactly what to say? Have you ever needed something and didn't know what to pray for? The Spirit of God prays perfectly and will help us when we run out of words to say. Therefore, when you finish praying in and with your understanding, try praying in the Spirit.

> *"Likewise the Spirit also helpeth our infirmities for we know not what we should pray for as we ought; but the Spirit makes intercessions for us with groaning which cannot be uttered."* (ROMANS 8:26)

I remember wanting to receive the Spirit of God because I considered myself a Christian, but I knew that I did not have the Spirit of God. The Word of God convicted me.

> *"And these signs shall follow them that believe."*
> (MARK 16:17A)

I said, "Lord, I believe. Why can't I do these things?"

He said, *Because you have not received them.*

I began to seek the Spirit of God. I began to go to churches where they said the Spirit of God dwelled. However, instead of the Spirit of God, I found "religion." Religion is man's attempt to worship God. Many churches do not know how to operate by the Spirit of God. They have certain rituals that they do to make it appear as though something spiritual is going on, but the build-up comes to nothing in the end. At the end of services, the people leave empty with their expectations shattered. I was very disappointed and very desperate to find the real Spirit of God.

One evening after returning home from church, my wife, Virginia, and I prayed to receive the Spirit of God. We did not want to get caught up in the rituals of some churches and not really receive the Spirit of God. We asked the Lord to forgive us of our sins and to give us His Spirit—we waited for something to happen. When it appeared as though nothing was happening, I prayed within myself to God and asked, "Why didn't anything happen?"

God asked me, *Do you believe?*

I said, "Yes, Lord."

He said, *Did you receive?*

I said, "Yes, Lord."

He said, *Well, praise me.*

We began to say, "Thank you, Jesus! Praise you, Jesus!" As we were praising Him, the Holy Ghost came upon us, we spoke in tongues, and we prayed for others all night long.

I realized that after praying to receive things from God, it is important to give Him praise. Praise is confirmation that you receive what you prayed for.

Let us pray.

Father in the name of Jesus, forgive us for our sins, and give us your Holy Spirit. We thank you, Lord, and we give You praise!

CHAPTER 3

Hearing His Voice

"My sheep hear my voice and I know them and they follow me." (JOHN 10:2)

After they accept Jesus as Lord over their life, many people wonder what the next step is. God said in His Word,

"In all thy ways acknowledge Him, and He will direct your path!" (PROVERBS 3:6)

Some new Christians look at others and follow their example, usually falling into misunderstanding and not really hearing from God. Jesus said,

"My sheep hear my voice and a stranger they will not follow." (JOHN 10:27)

One primary thing that is important for a Christian to learn is how to recognize the Voice of the Lord. There is a true and living Jesus that talks back to us and gives us instructions on what to do.

Some Christians think that God is in some far and distant place or that when you pray it is a one-way conversation and He'll answer in some type of code that needs to be interpreted. Since Jesus shed His blood on Calvary and paid the price for sin, He made it possible for us to find fellowship in the Father. Jesus called us His friend in John 15:15. I speak to my friends, and they speak back. But when God starts speaking, Satan also begins to speak, so you need to know the Voice of God or you will be misled.

> *"Beloved, believe not every spirit, but try the spirits whether they are of God."* (1 JOHN 4:1A)

When I first began to recognize the Voice of God, I became confused because I didn't know whether it was me and my thoughts or the devil. So I told Jesus that He should say, "In the Name of Jesus" before and "In the Name of Jesus" after speaking to me until I got familiar with His voice. Sometimes people say, "Something told me to do something," but it really was one of three persons: God, Satan, or yourself. God will direct your path and comfort and guide you. But the devil usually comes with a question, a suggestion, or a conflicting statement that is usually not in line with the Bible. But sometimes Satan uses parts of the Scripture that can be misinterpreted when taken out of context.

> *"Cast yourself from this Pinnacle for it is written, He has given the angels charge over thee."* (MATTHEW 4:6)

The Lord showed me the difference between Jesus, myself, and the devil. Many Christians pray but don't wait for the

CHAPTER 3: HEARING HIS VOICE

answer. They just say what they want and hope that God will answer. But God is a prayer-answering God! The next time you pray, you should first thank God, ask Him for your desire, then wait for Him to answer you—and He will.

"He who waits on the Lord He shall renew your strength." (ISAIAH 40:31)

The old patriots in the Bible heard the Voice of God. Abraham, Moses, Elisha, Isaiah, and Paul heard the Voice of the Lord, but they also took heed and obeyed His Voice. Many people and every Christian hear the Voice of the Lord, but they just don't obey it. The Word of God says,

"Be ye doers of the Word and not hearers only." (JAMES 1:22)

Sometimes people look for a lot of theatrics from God, like a light shining from the sky or an angel flying by. Most of the time, though, the Lord speaks to our hearts to tells us His Will. Have you ever been tempted to do something wrong, but something inside of you tells you not to do it? That is the Voice of God. Have you heard a voice telling you to do that wrong thing, and ask for forgiveness later? That is the voice of the devil.

Again, your voice ponders the question of which voice to yield to, saying "I want to, but I shouldn't," and that is you. We often don't listen to the Voice of God, we just do what feels right at that time.

The Word of God says,

> *"If you will hear His Voice, harden not your heart."*
> (HEBREWS 3:15)

After the Lord speaks to us, it is important that we listen and do what He tells us to do.

Have you ever been in church and it seems as if the preacher is preaching directly to you? The Lord uses the minister to speak to us also. But we get in the routine of going to church and wind up taking the Word of God for granted. The Word is sent forth every time the preacher or minister preaches. However, we look at it as though the message is the minister's interpretation. The Word of God says,

> *"No Scripture is for any private interpretation, for the Word was given by the Holy Men as the Holy Ghost moved on them."* (II PETER 1:21)

There are times when the people of God yield themselves to the Spirit of God. God will speak to you by a Word of Prophecy. *Lord, I feel empty and so defeated, but I know there is victory in you. I seem to have lost my place—please put me back where I am supposed to be and guide me completely. I yield myself to you—put me in your perfect will. Lord, I just want to be pleasing in your sight. If I am exalted, humble me. I don't want to get there before you. I know all things are possible with you. Let your perfect will be done in my life. Please forgive me for moving too hastily or according to my own will. Please let me get back in harmony with you. Let your spirit fall upon me and guide me to the way that you want me to go. Not my will, but your will. I just want to know you and to let other people know that there is peace, joy, and deliverance in your presence, Lord. Please bring your presence around me and show me how to follow your lead.*

He sent apostles, prophets, pastors, teachers, and evangelists for the perfecting of the saints and for the edifying of the body of Christ.

> *"Till we all come into the unity of the faith, and of the knowledge of the Son of God, unto a perfect man, unto the measure of the stature of the fullness of Christ."* (EPHESIANS 4:13)

Sometimes the Lord has key personnel to speak a specific Word to you. For example, when the Lord speaks a Word to your heart, you may or may not have understood it. He might send someone to you and speak that very same Word to you to confirm your understanding.

I remember when I first got saved for real. I was getting ready to go to summer camp, and a man that looked like he was crippled spoke to me and said, "Good afternoon."

I replied, "How are you doing?"

Then he looked at me and asked me what I was going to do.

I said, "Nothing much."

He said, "You are going to preach the Gospel—that's what you are going to do."

I was astonished! The Lord had recently spoken to my heart about preaching the Gospel, and this handicapped individual confirmed it to me again.

How effective your walk with Christ will be is dependent upon how much time you spend together and how much you share with one another. In order to establish trust, you have to know one another and talk to each other. The Word of God says,

> *"Draw nigh unto me I will draw nigh unto you."*
> (JAMES 4:8)

Jesus is so kind that He will not force His conversation on you; He will come when He is invited.

CHAPTER 4

A Call to Obedience

"I beseech you therefore, brethren, by the mercies of God, that ye present your bodies a living sacrifice, holy and acceptable to God, which is your reasonable service. And be not conformed to this world, but be ye transformed by the renewing of your mind that you may prove what is that good, and acceptable, and perfect will of God." (ROMANS 12:1-2)

The Lord has called us to be obedient to His Word. By being obedient to God's Word, we will be performing one of the greatest works that Jesus spoke about. Jesus said,

"I will not do anything except I go to Father."
(JOHN 5:19)

One of the greatest works that Jesus did was to obey the Word. Most people overlook this work, but it is important. By obeying the Word, you are obeying God.

> *"For there are three that bear record in heaven, the Father, the Word, and the Holy Ghost: and these three are one."* (JOHN 5:7)

Jesus is the Word made flesh, and to obey God's Word is to obey Jesus Himself. When we take the first step towards becoming a Christian, we acknowledge Jesus as Lord over our lives. Saying Jesus is Lord means that you will obey and do what He instructs you to do. The Word of God declares that if you acknowledge the Lord, He will direct your path. (Proverbs 3:6)

There is a band of Christians who believe that we will never be able to do what the Word says, so they don't try—besides we are only human. But Jesus was a man full of the Holy Ghost, and He obeyed. He was our example. So, instead of not putting forth an honest effort, we should get equipped with the same armor as Jesus and get full of the Holy Ghost. Then we will have the potential to do the same things that Jesus did. It is Jesus' nature to obey, and we are partakers of His divine nature. (2 Peter 1:1-4)

When Adam disobeyed God in the Garden of Eden, he broke the chain of obedience that was established by God. As a result, the Lord cursed the Earth and death entered the scene. But, by obeying God's Word, Jesus re-established the chain of obedience that was broken by Adam. Jesus proved that He was of God by having righteous fruit.

Some people say that holiness is the way to heaven. But Christ is the way to holiness. You cannot live a holy life without the Holy Ghost. Paul said, "I am crucified with Christ but nevertheless I live but not I, but Christ that lives in me. The life I live, I live by the faith of the Son of God who loves me and gave His life for me." (Galatians 2:20)

If you take Christ out of "Christian" you would have I-A-N; which means I Ain't Nothing! But if you put Christ into man, you get a righteous seed, a doer of the Word, for they are partakers of His Spirit and have the ability to do the Will of God.

> *"What shall we say then? Shall we continue in sin, that grace may abound? God forbid. How shall we, that are dead to sin, live any longer therein? Know ye not that so many of us were baptized into Jesus Christ were baptized into His death? Therefore, we are buried with Him in baptism into death: that like as Christ was raised up from the dead by the Glory of the Father, even so we also should walk in the newness of life. As we accept Christ we also accept the newness of life."* (ROMANS 6:1-4)

Since Jesus died on the cross at Calvary for our sins, the body of sin was destroyed. And when Jesus rose on the third day, He rose in the newness of life. As we accept Christ we also accept the newness of life. And if we let the Spirit of Christ rule in our lives, we will not obey the lust of the flesh. Of course you will be tempted, but you don't have to yield to that temptation.

> *"Let not sin therefore reign in your mortal body, that you should obey it in the lust thereof."* (ROMANS 6:12)

> *"For he that is dead is freed from sin. Now if we be dead with Christ, we believe that we should also live with Him."* (ROMANS 6:7-8)

> *"Knowing this that our old man is crucified with Him, that the body of sin might be destroyed, that henceforth we should not serve sin."* (ROMANS 6:6)

I have seen many people rely on His mercy and completely disregard obeying the Word of God. But the Word of God declares,

> *"If you are willing and obedient, you shall eat the good of the land. But if you refuse and rebel you shall be devoured by the sword; for the mouth of the Lord has spoken it."* (ISAIAH 1:19-20)

He that said

> *"I know Him and does not keep His commandments, is a liar, and the truth is not in him. But whosoever keeps His Word, in him verily is the love of God perfected: hereby we know that we are in Him. He that says he abides in Him himself should walk as He walked."* (1 JOHN 2:4-6)

So Jesus wants us to come into the fullness of His Grace. He wants us to press toward being as He is. We can, if we have continued fellowship with God. The more time you spend with Jesus, the more you become like Him.

> *"Till we all come to the unity of the faith, and of the knowledge of the Son of God, to a perfect man, to the measure of the stature of the fullness of Christ."*
> (EPHESIANS 4:13)

Let God be our mark for what is right and press toward it! Some people believe they may not be able to live up to that standard. But it is not you that is doing the living. Remember, Jesus substituted His life for our life at the cross. He took the death that we should have because of all the sins of the world. He gave us His life through and through, and we are partakers of His divine nature.

> *"Now you are clean through the Word which I have spoken to you. Abide in me and I in you. As the branch cannot bear fruit of itself, except it abides in the vine; no more can you, except you abide in me."* (JOHN 15:3-4)

You cannot live right unless you stay in Jesus. Some people think that it is so hard to do what God says and it is hard outside of the Holy Ghost. Jesus said,

> *"If you continue in my Word then you are my true disciples."* (JOHN 8:31B)

After we find out what sin is and where it is in our lives according to the Word of God, we should not continue to practice it. There has to be a stopping point; there has to be a point of repentance. The Word of God declares that,

> *"If we confess our sins, He is faithful and just to forgive us our sins, and to cleanse us from all unrighteousness."* (1 JOHN 1:8-9)

> *"Though your sins may be as scarlet I will wash them whiter than snow."* (ISAIAH 1:18)

Don't let this opportunity for a new beginning and a clean start pass you by.

Let us pray, remember confess with your mouth and believe in your heart, and ye shall be saved.

Father, in the name of Jesus, we acknowledge that we have sinned. Please forgive us for sinning against you. We accept you as Lord and Savior in our lives. In the name of Jesus, direct my path. I accept your guidance, Lord. Guide me completely out of sin. Thank you, Jesus. Praise your Holy Name. Jesus, Jesus, Jesus, Jesus, Jesus, Jesus, Jesus—thank you.

CHAPTER 5

Cleaning out the Closet

"Let us therefore as many be perfect or mature be thus minded; and if in anything ye be other minded, God shall reveal even this unto you." (PHILIPPIANS 3:14)

"Every branch in me that beareth not fruit he taketh away; and every branch that beareth fruit he purgeth it, that it may bring forth more fruit." (JOHN 15:2)

Have you ever seen a plant that has just begun to grow? Most of the time, if the plant is in the ground, in order for it to grow effectively, you will have to pull all the weeds from around it. And if the plant has any dead parts, those parts are cut off so that the plant can continue to grow and bear fresh leaves.

Jesus does the same for us. Jesus wants us to come as we are because He knows we cannot change ourselves. But after we accept Jesus as Lord, He begins to point out things in our lives that need to be changed if we are to come into the fullness of the statute of God.

I have heard many Christians say that you can live any kind of way—the grace of God will cover it. However, the Word of God says that after you come in the knowledge of God, there remains no forgiveness for sin. In other words, if you continue to sin after you know that it is sin, there can be no more forgiveness.

Jesus will reveal to you the things that are not pleasing to Him and He will instruct you to renounce them. We all know that God knows all about us. So He can see us even on the inside. God knows about all of the sins we have committed, and He knows all of our habits. He can reveal even the secret sins that are deep in the closet—the sins that only God and you can see. The Word of God says that everything that is done in the dark shall be brought to the light. (Luke 12:2,3)

I have seen Christians who say, "I know that it is wrong, but the Lord will forgive me." By saying that you are a Christian yet are not doing what it takes either outwardly or inwardly, you are making the Word of God a lie.

I always wonder why God wants us to confess our sins. God already knows what I did wrong, so why would I have to tell Him? It is true that God knows all of us, but He is giving us an opportunity to get the lie out ourselves. God wants us to put all the cards on the table. He wants us to be honest with Him and, the world, and ourselves. There are no lies in God, so He does not want any lies in you. Remember, what the Word says in Revelation 21:8:

CHAPTER 5: CLEANING OUT THE CLOSET

"All liars will have their part in the lake which burns with fire and brimstone, which is the second death."

After I got saved "for real", the Lord began to point out the things in my life that He wanted me to renounce. He was specific because He knew that I wanted to be saved for real this time. I was half-saved for years, but half-saved is not saved at all. I was going to church on Sunday but living a sinful life the rest of the week with the understanding that the Lord knew my heart, and I was not as bad as most. I kept saying, "At least I am going to church. The Lord is merciful." Not so! We should not use God's mercy as a cloak to hide sin as though I can ask the Lord for forgiveness when I get through sinning.

The Lord is calling us not only to accept the forgiveness of God because it is given, but to repent and not to continue in sin. If I was a thief, after I accept Christ and repent from my sin for real, allowing Christ to rule in my life, I should not steal any more. The Word of God said,

"Ye shall know them by their fruit." (MATTHEW 7:16)

To be a true Christian is to live a life of integrity.

I conducted a survey of approximately 200 people and asked five questions:

- What does it mean to be honest?
- What does it mean to be accountable?

- What does it mean to be responsible?
- What does it mean to have integrity?
- Do you think it is possible to live honestly?

I was truly surprised by the responses I received. Most people did not believe that anyone could live honestly or without lying. They believe that it is impossible to live an effective Christian life if you are not honest with yourself and God. It is impossible to live a life of integrity without living honestly. Everything comes out and nothing will be a secret. Remember, God sees all and knows all from the inside out. He wants us to live honestly from the inside out.

> *"Beloved, now are we the sons of God, and it doth not yet appear what we shall be: but we know that, when He shall appear, we shall be like Him; for we shall see Him as He is. And every man that hath this hope in Him purifieth himself, even as He is pure."*
> (1 JOHN 3: 2-3)

If we are looking for His blessed appearance, we must let the Holy Ghost cleanse us so that we may be without spot or blemish. But what are the things that can cleanse us? Abiding in the Word, living by the Word, and

> *"The anointing which ye have received of Him abideth in you, and ye need not that any man teach you: but as the same anointing teacheth you all things, and is truth, and is no lie, and even as it hath taught you, you shall abide in Him."* (1 JOHN 2:27)

CHAPTER 5: CLEANING OUT THE CLOSET

"Now ye are clean through the Word which I have spoken unto you. Abide in me, and I in you. As the branch cannot bear fruit of itself, except it abide in the vine; no more can ye except ye abide in me. I am the vine, ye are the branches: He that abideth in me, and I in him, the same bringeth forth much fruit: for without me ye can do nothing." (JOHN 15:3-5)

Let us pause for a moment of prayer.

Father, in name of Jesus, show us how to abide in you. Show us how to yield to your Word. Show us how to fellowship with your Spirit. In the name of Jesus, we submit our whole heart unto you from us to your liking. Show us how to be honest with you and with ourselves. In the name of Jesus, we yield our complete soul and spirit unto you. We receive you totally as Lord over our affairs, as Lord over our finances, as Lord over every decision we make. Show us how to walk according to your Word. In the name of Jesus, we pray. Amen. Thank you, Jesus! Praise God! Praise you, Jesus! Jesus! Jesus!

CHAPTER 6

A Call to Service

"But ye shall receive power, after that the Holy Ghost is come upon you: and ye shall be witnesses unto me both in Jerusalem, and in all Judaea, and in Samaria, and unto the uttermost part of the earth." (ACTS 1:8)

Now, after getting saved "for real" and becoming filled with the Spirit of God, most Christians think that they are only supposed to attend church until Jesus comes back. Yes, you are supposed to attend church. However, the Lord did not give you all that power to just sit in a church.

While you are at church only receiving the Word, there are millions of people who are starving for the Word of God. The harvest is truly great, but the laborers are few. After the apostles received the Holy Ghost in the upper room, they changed the world. They began to proclaim Christ everywhere they went. They were not ashamed; they were bold. Even in the face of death, they proclaimed Christ.

Most of us will go to a certain level with Christ, but then begin to second-guess ourselves, saying, "The Lord did not call me to do that," or "I am not qualified." But the Word of God says in Mark 16:15,

> *"Go ye into all the World and preach the gospel to every creature."*

> *"All power is given unto me in heaven and in earth. Go ye therefore, and teach all nations, baptizing them in the name of the Father, and of the Son, and of the Holy Ghost: Teaching them to observe all things whatsoever I have commanded you: and, lo I am with you always, even unto the end of the world. Amen."* (MATTHEW 28:18B-20).

Jesus did not intend for us to just receive the Word. After he saved us and washed us, He called us into His service to be witnesses unto Him. Of course you can witness by living the Christian life in front of people, but, in living a Christian life, you will have to also tell people about the doctrine of Jesus.

The Word of God says,

> *"I will send Him unto you the Comforter, the Holy Ghost. And when He comes He will reprove the world of sin, and of righteousness, and of judgment."* (JOHN 16:8)

After the Spirit of God comes in the way that the Bible says, you cannot help but to tell somebody about what God is doing in your life. Most sinners do not mind telling you what is going on in their lives. They are eager to share that they stayed out all night drinking and had such a good time doing wrong that was not according to the Word. Yet we Christians sometime feel intimidated by them. So we do not tell them of the goodness of Jesus or guide them out of trouble through the Word. We are even afraid of correcting someone when they are wrong. We use the excuse, "I would say something, but I do not want to offend them." It is better for them to be offended for a little while than not to be offended and go to hell happy. There are thousands of people dying and going to hell every day because some Christians have not led them to Christ.

It is every Christians' ministry to witness for Christ and show this world who Jesus is. Of course you will be persecuted, but some will believe and receive the Word of God from you. Remember, the servant is not higher than the master. If they persecuted Christ, they will persecute you.

> *"As ye go, preach, saying, 'The kingdom of heaven is at hand.' Heal the sick, cleanse the lepers, raise the dead, cast out devils: freely ye have received, freely give."*
> (MATTHEW 10:7-8)

In other words, you have received the Word of God freely, so it is time to give back. Remember, everything reproduces after its own kind. Monkeys produce monkeys; birds produce birds; liars produce liars. Most people will try to convince you that it is okay to do what they are doing. True Christians produce true Christians. The Word of God is the incorruptible seed of life.

Have you ever read the parable of the Sower? It is found in Mark's 4th chapter, Matthew's 13th chapter, and Luke's 8th chapter. The Sower sowed the Word. He sows the Word to everybody—good ground, bad ground, unsure ground, and misunderstood ground. The main concern of the Sower was to get the Word out. He witnessed to all of them—even to the ones who did not understand. They knew that He was the Sower. He did not pick the ground he sowed; as the Lord led, he sowed.

We are supposed to be the Sowers of God's Word into the hearts of men. God is the husbandman of the farmer—the one who tilled the ground and turned the dirt over. If the ground is tilled but there is no seed, there will be no harvest. We are to proclaim Christ everywhere we go in words, in action, in work habits, and in witnessing. When they see you, they will know that you are different.

In the same chapters, Jesus says that no man lights a candle and puts it under a bushel, but on a candlestick. We should let our light so shine that others will see our good works and glorify God.

The Word of God also says,

> *"But if the watchman see the sword come, and blow not the trumpet, and the people be not warned; if the*

> *sword come, and take any person form among them, he is taken away in his iniquity; but his blood will I require at the watchman's hand. So thou, O son of man, I have set thee a watchman unto the house of Israel; therefore thou shall hear the Word at my mouth, and warn them from me."* (EZEKIEL 33:6-7)

We are accountable for telling the good news, and if we don't, the blood is required at our hand. If you were to see a house on fire and saw someone walking towards the house, you would scream to them, "Do not go in there! There is a fire!" You might even physically prevent them from entering the burning building. People who do not know Jesus as Lord are essentially doing the same thing, but their fire is an eternal fire in hell. The words that you speak to them might change their lives and save their souls from destruction. There is a serious penalty for not accepting Jesus as Lord; it is a penalty that no one should have to suffer since Jesus took the punishment for us.

> *"The Lord is not slack concerning His promise, as some men count slackness; but is longsuffering to us-ward, not willing that any should perish, but that all should come to repentance."* (2 PETER 3:9)

God created hell for Satan and the other rebellious angels who followed him. But whosoever follows Satan's way shall have the same fate as him. Can you sit and watch as a child hurts himself? Most of the time we will try to prevent it. And if he falls, we will help him up and comfort him. Jesus wants us to do the same towards one another. Help others to reach Jesus before it is too late.

CHAPTER 7

Personal Instructions

"For as many are led by the Spirit of God, they are the sons of God." (ROMANS 8:14)

It is good to have a God who will personally lead you through this life. After you receive Jesus as Lord in your life, He will personally lead you to victory. He will give you instructions every step of the way. The Word of God says that if you acknowledge Him, He will direct your path. There is much to be done in this life. The Lord is coming back, and we want to be ready. But we also want to get as many other people ready with us as possible. I believe that when the Lord saved us, He did not intend for us to sit around having meetings until He comes but to reclaim the kingdom and occupy it until He comes.

Where do we begin? There is so much to be done. Some people may start without receiving instructions from the Lord. Remember: if you acknowledge Him, he will direct your path. We have to acknowledge Him. (Proverbs 3:6)

The Lord will give you personal instructions on what He wants you to do if you acknowledge Him. How can we acknowledge Him? If it is done in faith, praying a sincere and honest prayer will touch the heart of God. For the righteousness of God is revealed from faith to faith. As it is written, the just shall live by faith. Most people do not spend time praying or in fellowship with God. The more you are around someone and talk to them, the more you get to know them personally. Most people do not know what God wants from them because they do not ask Him.

I remember once when I was in Hattiesburg, Mississippi, I was passing out Bibles and telling people to repent and turn to Jesus. I met a guy who used to be a preacher. I asked him what had made him stop preaching, and he said that he had lost everything he had, including his wife. So he had decided that he was wasting his time. I asked him what had made him start preaching. He responded, "A strong feeling."

He had started on his own. However, if the Lord calls you to preach, you will know it—He will tell you himself. He started preaching not because he was instructed by God, but because he had a feeling. It is always best to hear it from God in your heart. "For you shall know the truth, and the truth shall make you free." (John 8:32) The Lord gave personal instructions to everyone in the Bible, so why would be different? Maybe you do not like what God has told you to do—do it anyway! Remember: God can see everything from all sides. Perhaps He is seeing something that you are not seeing. Maybe, it is God's way of re-establishing the chain of obedience.

Pray and seek God's guidance, and He will guide you step by step. God will not tell you to do anything that you could not do. And he said,

> *"He will never leave you nor forsake you."*
> (DEUTERONOMY 31:6)

And He is faithful to His Word. As much as possible, you should set aside a time to pray and fellowship with God. The more you are around Him, the more you understand Him.

> *"Draw nigh unto me I will draw nigh to unto you."*
> (JAMES 4:8)

> *"The footsteps of a righteous man are ordered by God."*
> (PSALM 37:23)

Remember, after Jesus rose from the dead, He met His disciples and opened their understanding that they might understand the Scriptures (Luke 24:45). He then gave them personal instructions, telling them to go and spread the Gospel and the Word of God. They went forth and preached everywhere. The Lord was working with them, confirming the Word with signs (Mark 16:20). The Lord will not send you out unprepared, and He will not send you out alone. He will personally go with you to confirm the Word as you preach with signs and miracles following.

Wherever the anointed Word of God is preached, miracles and signs will follow it. Jesus will prove His Word to be true. He will not make you ashamed. Sometimes when I am preaching, the Lord will tell me to walk from side to side or walk to the back and guide me word by word through the sermon. I remember once when the Lord woke me up at night, telling me to pray for a girl named Tamekia. I did not know a Tamekia, but I prayed in obedience to God. The next morning I read in the newspaper about three different girls named Tamekia—one had been shot, one had been in a fire, and another had meningitis. From that time on, I promised that I would never hesitate when the Lord tells me to do something.

He will give you personal instructions pertaining to your life or to benefit someone else. The Lord will not leave you in limbo, wondering what you should do. He will tell you and show you step by step. He will work with you. Many people have started churches and movements, not because the Lord told them to, but because they were not satisfied with what was going on in their home churches. Instead of praying about the situation or asking for God's guidance, they acted for themselves—that is one reason why there are so many different denominations.

It is very important to pray and seek God's guidance—do it before you do anything else. It is very important to keep your close, special relationship with God intact. Remember: the more you engage in fellowship with Him, the more you will know Him. My mother used to say, "You will never know someone until you live with them." The Word says if you abide within Me and my Words abide in you, you can ask what ye will and it shall be done unto you. (John 15:7)

CHAPTER 8

A Call to Service

He gave some apostles, some prophets, and some evangelist, and some pastors, and some teachers; For the perfecting of the saints, for the work of the ministry, for the edifying of the body of Christ, till we all come into the unity of the faith, and the knowledge of the Son of God, until a perfect measure of the stature of the fullness of Christ. (EPHESIANS 4:11-13)

In the body of Christ, The Lord has called some to nurture young Christians through the growing process. God understands where you are as a Christian, whether you are a new convert or well-seasoned in the Word. At each level in your Christian walk, the Lord will send a leader or a guide into your life to lead you as you grow into the person God wants you to be. In Ephesians 4:11, the Bible states five ministries, and in the book of Titus it mentions two appointed offices—the Bishop and the deacon. In other verses it mentions the usher and the missionary.

When God allows you to be in position to lead and guide His people, it is a serious matter. You have their eternal soul opened, willing to be filled with the information that you give them with the understanding that the instructions are coming from God. Therefore, sanctify yourself when you are put over His people so you can receive from God not mixed with our opinion. The vessel of God must be clean and purified so the Word can be delivered with clarity.

Make yourself available to hear from God. The Word of God states,

> *"My sheep hear My voice and I know them and they follow me."* (JOHN 10:27)

When followers come to church, they are coming to hear the voice of God. They are not coming to hear clever speeches or cheerful inspiration. They want deliverance from the oppression of life, and Jesus is the only way to true deliverance. Jesus said,

> *"I am the way, the truth, and the life—no man comes to the Father but by Me."* (JOHN 14:6)

Leading God's people can be very challenging without His guiding hand. We all have certain personalities that can have an effect on the leader's leadership style. It is important to realize how we administer the service of The Lord as leaders of God's people—it cannot be based on our opinion, feelings, or emotions. We should get our information from God so the people of God can get unfiltered revelations from

Him. Don't get me wrong—you should be passionate about sharing information that God is giving you and His people. However, we should not allow our personal thoughts or feelings dictate how we lead.

> *"Trust in The Lord with all your heart and lean not to your own understanding. In all thy ways acknowledge Him and He shall direct your path."* (PROVERBS 3:5-6)

God wants us to come to Him for guidance. He loves us so much that He does not want us to make mistakes. Mistakes happen when we lean on our own understanding and fail to go to God, who can see every angle of any situation. Although God has instruction and guidance available for us, He does not force us to take it. He gives us autonomy and free will to make decisions on our own. But remember, there are consequences to our actions.

The ministry of Jesus Christ is equipped to reach, teach, and develop individuals to be the type of people who God wants us to be—ready to serve, fervent in prayer, constant in worship, moving toward leadership, and ready to grow.

An Apostle is a "sent one"—a vigorous and pioneering advocate or supporter of a particular policy, idea, or cause. An Apostle is sent by God to establish and organize the church, ordain elders, be the spiritual authority in the body of Christ and extend God's influence over the land. An Apostle establishes disciples (disciplined followers of Christ) and mentors leaders. An Apostle is supposed to be the point of accountability for leaders. An Apostle gives true spiritual guidance to leaders and empowers pastors to feed the flock. An Apostle operates in the Spirit as the Lord leads and encourages the leaders to operate in the gifts of the Spirit also.

The Spiritual gifts are the weapons that are not carnal, that pull down strongholds (2 Corinthians 10:4). An Apostle should encourage leaders to teach about spiritual gifts, spiritual warfare, righteousness, and how to apply the Word to daily living. The Apostle should mentor their leaders on how to respond to adversity and how to be led by the Spirit constantly. After an Apostle establishes the church and ordains elders, they should move on to the next work as the Lord leads. This will allow the leaders to do what they were trained to do and operate in their position freely. The Apostle should go back and check on the development of the established church, but if they stay too long, it could give way to confusion. The new leader needs to have the freedom to operate as the Lord leads. The Apostle must have a sure word from God. To walk in this way will require them to spend time before God in His Holy presence until they are one with Him.

The Bishop of a church is a minister of the highest order appointed to organize administrative functions in the churches, supervise leaders, and give spiritual guidance. A Bishop must have experience in the church, must be blameless as the steward of God, not be self-willed, not be quick to anger, not be given to wine, not be a striker, not be money-hungry, be a lover of hospitality, support good men, and be sober, just, holy, and temperate (self-controlled). He must hold fast to the faith that he has been taught, so that he may be able to exhort and to convince the gainsayer through sound doctrine. The Bishop should have one wife and faithful children who cannot be accused of being unruly (Titus 1:6-9). The Bishop should be the example of how a leader should act publicly and privately. A Bishop encourages the body of Christ and should motivate them to keep the Word of God and live it daily. The Bishop should be an example of how the applied Word of God looks daily, giving no place to the devil and staying focused on the mission that God has for the church. The Bishop should be approachable and easy to talk to. The Bishop should use words with discretion; the Bishop's words can affect the whole ministry.

A Prophet is God's spokesperson, hearing directly from God's mouth. The Prophet's job is to communicate the plan of God to the body of Christ. Sometimes a Prophet is used to give a personal word from God to individuals and leaders of the church, but the office of the Prophet is to speak God's vision to the body of Christ. God operates through Prophets with clarity when the vessel is clean and not looking for self gain. A Prophet is chosen by God to be sanctified and is separated so that they might hear God's voice without being contaminated with worldly views. God uses Prophets to warn His people to repent of their sin and turn to the path of righteousness. Prophets are also used to encourage the body of Christ and give a blessed hope to the congregation, to motivate them to stay strong and complete the mission that God has for their life. Being a Prophet is more than giving a word of knowledge. The manifestation of the Spirit is given to every man to profit with all (1 Corinthians 12:7). If it's needed for the body, God can use anybody to accomplish the mission of His Word. Just because the Spirit of God comes upon you and you give a Word of prophecy does not necessarily mean you hold the office of a Prophet. The anointing of God rests on a Prophet and the Prophet's voice is constant and available to God at all times. Sometimes being a Prophet is lonely on the human side because of the abundance of the revelations Gods share with them with clarity. They might want to share this information from God but cannot because it is classified, confidential information from God that can only be delivered at the right time when God says to do so. The Prophet must truly watch their speech and not speak hastily or out of wrath. A true Prophet's words come to pass. Therefore, a Prophet must exercise temperance (self control) because the actions of a true Prophet can have consequences that can change the atmosphere. Elijah spoke and said that it would not rain until he said so, and it did not rain for three years and six months; when he spoke again the rain came (1 Kings 17:1) (James 5:17). Sometimes the enemy will try to provoke a Prophet to speak a Word that God has given him before the time or to say something out of anger, but the Prophet needs to stay focused on the will of God and respond only when God commands him to.

In the body of Christ, the Prophet is important for strategic moves and church. In order to have an impact on the community, they need a Word from the Lord. The Prophet clearly explains to the church what direction God wants them to move. Timing is important when it comes to the move of God. A true Prophet can become a false prophet if they let their opinions and views lead them. The Spirit of God will move out if He is grieved, and the spirit of divination will come in. It will seem as if nothing has changed because the "Prophet" can still see some things that will come to pass, but it is not of God—be careful!

> *"Many shall say to me in that day, 'Lord we prophesied in your name, and cast out devils in your name, did many wonderful works in your name', then I will profess to them, 'I never knew you; depart from me ye that work iniquity.'"* (MATTHEW 7:22,23)

Iniquity is sin that you know is sin yet do anyway, sometimes secretly. That should be a scary scripture for all church leaders and should make you examine yourself to make sure you are in good standing with God. There are ways that may seem right to a man, but the end is the way of destruction (Proverbs 14:12).

A Pastor is the heart of the body of Christ. The Pastor is like a farmer who plants the seed that is the Word of God (Matthew 8:3) into believers and those who could be believers. The Pastor takes care of the garden of believers, removing weeds from around them, watering them, putting fertilizer around them, and encouraging them to grow. The Pastor nurtures the new believers, giving them every opportunity to grow. A Pastor must be patient with the people of God and be very approachable; they should have a calm demeanor. The Pastor must not allow the crowd to sway them but be steadfast in the Word. The Pastor must be sanctified and separated so that God can give them His Word and so he can share the peoples' heart to God. The Pastor must be a student of the Word and a good steward over God's business.

The Pastor must be filled with the Spirit of God to understand God's heart and to have the God type of compassion. The Pastor should also be a protector of the souls that God allows them to watch over, ensuring that they receive sound, easy-to-understand doctrine. Pastors should operate in the gifts of the Spirit as God lead. The Pastor must preach the Word in season and out of season (2 Timothy 4:2), teach righteousness, holiness, and how to live in the Word day to day. The Pastor should work in conjunction with city leaders and help the community come into harmony with the Word of God. The church should do complete community outreach to keep the flow of believers coming and growing to build up the body of Christ. The church should be the moral compass of the city—in doing so, it could help prevent crime.

The Evangelist and the Missionary should work together, hand in hand, to develop an outreach plan for the church. The Pastor should bless it and approve the plan before it is implemented. An Evangelist is a person who seeks to convert others to the Christian faith by preaching publicly. An Evangelist preaches the inspired Word of God, often in a revival setting, to convert nonbelievers to repentance and convince backsliding Christians to rededicate their lives to Christ. The Evangelist helps guide Christians to make a deeper commitment in their church. The Evangelist must be filled with the Holy Ghost, be consecrated, and be sanctified in order to be effective on the Christian battlefield. The Evangelist must spend time before God to get His pure, unadulterated Word. The Evangelist must stay in contact with the Pastor to ensure unity and cohesion in each phase of the ministry. The Evangelist leads the new converts to church so that the Pastor can nourish and mentor them on their Christian journey. Paul plants, Apollo waters, and God gives the increase (1 Corinthians 3:6).

The Missionary and the Evangelist should work together in the ministry. The Missionary Bible tracks and offers the churches service as it relates to social matters. The church should be involved in community outreach such as feeding the hungry, clothing the needy, mentoring the youth, educating and developing families, counseling marriages, and resolving conflict. The Evangelist and the Missionary should be the arms of outreach in the church. The church should show the love of Christ by being a living example of what to do and how to live in society. Don't love in word only, but in deed also (1 John 3:18). The Missionary is more of a grassroots-type worker in the ministry, showing the kindness of God in a hands-on way. By working hand in hand with the Evangelist, they can guide believers and nonbelievers to church where they can be taught the Word of God in a way that covers all doctrine, giving them a good foundation. The Missionary and the Evangelist show the love and kindness of the church to the world, which will promote church growth, love, and compassion.

The Teacher in the body is very important to the ministry's success. The Teacher should be well versed in the Word of God and able to explain any particulars. The teacher should be approachable and be able to communicate effectively in an easy-to-understand way. The teaching atmosphere should be conducive to questions and curiosity. The Teacher should be committed to studying the Bible and be willing to do research and find learning material to make learning easier. The Bible is the authority on all Christian teaching. All teaching material should line up with the Word of God that is the Bible. The Teacher should be filled with the Holy Ghost in order to rightly divide the Word of Truth.

> *"But God hath revealed them to us by the Spirit: for the Spirit searches all things, yea even the deep things of God."* (1 CORINTHIANS 2:10)

The Teacher should have a humble spirit and not be condescending toward the students. The Teacher should be prepared to encounter students with different learning abilities. Advanced learners should be given more challenging lessons to keep their minds from drifting, while intermediate learners and new converts should be taught slowly so they won't get overwhelmed and quit. The Word of God must be precept on precept, line upon line, here a little, and there a little (Isaiah 28:10). The teacher must stay before God's face in order to get a clear understanding of His Word. Study to show yourself approved unto God rightly dividing the Word of truth (2 Timothy 2:15). God is your audience, and God is the authority to approve your lesson plan. The lesson should be blessed by the Pastor to ensure that the church is on the same page.

The Usher is the church greeter and the doorkeeper to the church. The Usher can set the tone for the church service. When the Usher gives a warm greeting to visitors and church members, their caring attitude can make the congregation more receptive to the Word of God. The Usher should be a prayer warrior as they help usher the Spirit of God into the service.

The Deacons of the church also help with operations. The Deacons oversee the business and administrative portions of the church making sure bills are paid and repairs to the church are completed as needed. The Deacon should be well versed in the Word, be ready to teach, preach, and do anything else that is necessary to keep the church operational. The Pastor has to be in the presence of God to get the revelation of His Word, so Deacons were appointed to handle the day-to-day business of the church.

> *"Get from among ye seven men of honest report, full of the Holy Ghost and wisdom whom ye can appoint over this business."* (ACTS 6:3)

Some organizations think the Deacons are in charge of the Pastor, but that is not so. The Deacon and everyone else in the body is subject to the Pastor's authority, which is given by God.

Some denominations have removed the office of the Apostle and the Prophet from the church. They say that there is no need for those offices anymore. The Word of God states that those offices were given for the perfecting of the saints, for the work of the ministry, and for the edifying of the body till we all come into the unity of the faith of the knowledge of God, unto the perfect measure of the statue of the fullness of the Son of God (Ephesians 4:12,13). There is always a need for the body of Christ to be edified because we are always getting new believers and moving to different levels in God. There is always a need for all the offices God has placed in the body of Christ. In order to effectively fulfill the jobs God has called us to do, we must do it God's way.

CONCLUSION

A Higher Calling

When you receive Jesus as Lord and Savior in your life, it is only the beginning of your journey. You must follow the path you're led down by the Holy Ghost, which will develop you into the person God wants you to become. After you have been tried, you will be elevated to another level in Christ. But there is a price for walking in a higher calling. The price may be high, but the rewards are priceless. It is a great honor to be approved by God to guide His people through the Christian life and one that should not be taken lightly.

> *"This one thing I do I press toward the mark of the high calling of God in Christ Jesus."* (PHILIPPIANS 4:13,14)

God anoints His true disciples, which makes leaders effective in your life and in the lives of others. A leader should accept and embrace their calling so that their ministry and life can flow in accordance with the Word of God. In Matthew 11:28-30, Jesus said,

> *"Come unto me ye who are labored and heavy laden and I will give you rest. Take my yoke upon you and learn of me; I am meek and lowly in heart; and ye shall find rest for your soul. For my yoke is easy and my burden is light."*

The biggest barrier to the gospel is you. God wants us to humble ourselves and follow the path that was put before us by Jesus Christ. We have to put down our personal agenda and pick up the agenda God has set for our lives. To be anointed is to have God's approval to operate in His authority and with His ability. God's authority and God's ability will impact your life and the lives of others in a way that is explosive and creative. We have to let our hearts and minds be fine-tuned to the Spirit of God so that we are able to hear God with clarity. Hearing the Spirit will give you courage to execute God's will constantly. Jesus said,

> *"If anyone would come after me let him deny himself, take up the cross, and follow me."* (MATTHEW 16:24)

We should not put our own goals and desires in front of God's plans. He must be number one in our life! God must come before family and friends. God does not have a problem with you having goals and plans, but He just has to be Lord. Allow God to take the lead in your life. He knows what is in your path—just go to Him!

> *"In all thy way, acknowledge Him and He shall direct your path."* (PROVERB 3:5)

CONCLUSION: A HIGHER CALLING

Stay focused, yield to the Spirit of God, submit yourself to the leading of the Holy Ghost, and let Him have His way in your ministry. There is a higher calling in ministry and in life. The calling is to walk as Jesus did on the Earth. The calling is to do the same miracles that Jesus did with the same power.

> *"The works that I did, ye shall do also and greater works shall ye do because I go to the Father and whatsoever ye ask in my name, I will do it!"*
> (JOHN 14:12-14)

Let God escort you to the higher calling that He has for you in Jesus' name!

www.ingramcontent.com/pod-product-compliance
Lightning Source LLC
LaVergne TN
LVHW051036070526
838201LV00010B/225